To:

From:

Published by Sellers Publishing, Inc.
Copyright © 2018 Sellers Publishing, Inc.
All rights reserved.

Sellers Publishing, Inc.
161 John Roberts Road, South Portland, Maine 04106
Visit our Web site: www.sellerspublishing.com • E-mail: rsp@rsvp.com

Mary L. Baldwin, Managing Editor
Charlotte Cromwell, Production Editor
Compiled by Charlotte Cromwell
Cover and interior design by Charlotte Cromwell

Illustrations © 2018 Magnia/Shutterstock.com;
Markovka/Shutterstock.com; Nebula Cordata/Shutterstock.com;
Kat_Branch/Shutterstock.com; Floral Deco/Shutterstock.com;
Flaffy/Shutterstock.com.

ISBN 13: 978-1-4162-4641-1

10 9 8 7 6 5 4 3 2 1

Printed in China.

STRONG AS A MOTHER

you are amazing, you are brave, you are inspiring

SELLERS
PUBLISHING

Sometimes the
strength of
motherhood
is greater than
natural laws.

Barbara Kingsolver

To describe my mother would be to write about a hurricane in its perfect power. Or the climbing, falling colors of a rainbow.

≽Maya Angelou≼

Motherhood is 'heart-exploding,' blissful hysteria.'

≻Olivia Wilde≺

My mother . . . made me strong, but she wanted me to be strong. That's more important.

Diane von Furstenberg

It's not easy being a mother. If it were easy, fathers would do it.

>DOROTHY ON *The Golden Girls*‹

My mother . . . she is beautiful, softened at the edges and tempered with a spine of steel. I want to grow old and be like her.

➤Jodi Picoult➤

When you are a mother, you are never really alone in your thoughts. A mother always has to think twice, once for herself and once for her child.

⇒SOPHIA LOREN⇐

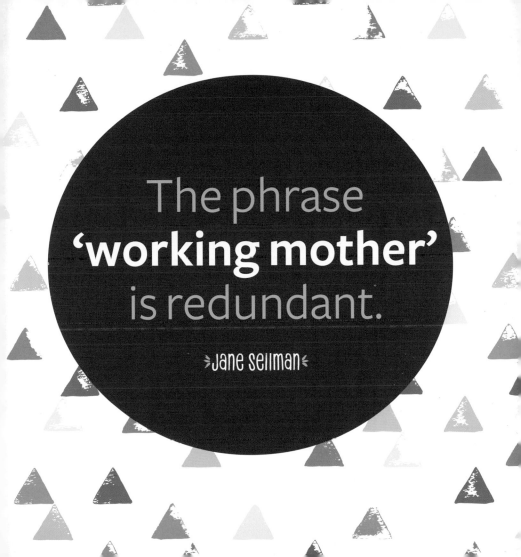

The phrase **'working mother'** is redundant.

⟩Jane Sellman⟨

Acceptance, tolerance, bravery, compassion. These are the things my mom taught me.

Lady Gaga

I think every working mom probably feels the same thing: You go through big chunks of time where you're just thinking, 'This is impossible — oh, this is impossible.' And then you **JUST KEEP GOING,** and keep going, and you sort of do the impossible.

Tina Fey

My mother's menu consisted of two choices: Take it or leave it.

>Buddy Hackett<

Being a **mother**
is learning about
strengths you didn't
know you had and
dealing with **fears** you
didn't know existed.

›Linda Wooten‹

When you're in the thick of raising your kids by yourself, you tend to keep a running list of everything you think you're doing wrong. I recommend taking a lot of family pictures as evidence to the contrary.

≫CONNIE SCHULTZ≪

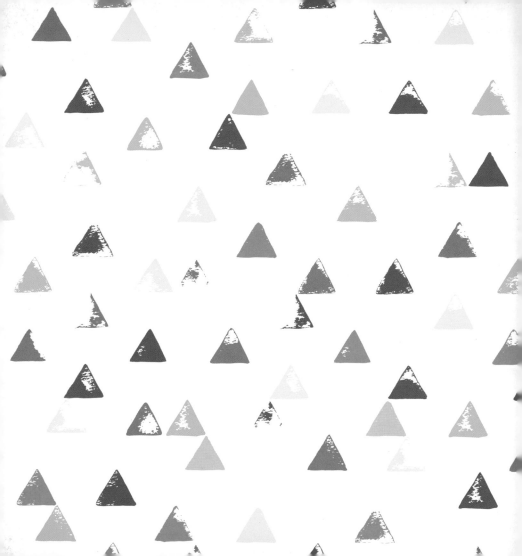

There's no way to be a perfect mother and a million ways to be a good one.

>Jill Churchill<

I would say that **my mother is the single biggest role model in my life**, but that term doesn't seem to encompass enough when I use it about her. She was the love of my life.

>Mindy Kaling<

Mothers were
the only ones you
could depend on to
tell the whole,
unvarnished truth.

⟩Margaret Dilloway⟨

A
mother is
the one who
fills your heart
in the first place.

>AMY TAN<

The word's out:
I'm a woman, and I'm going to have trouble backing off on that. I am what I am. I'll go out and talk to people about what's happening to their families, and when I do that, I'm a mother.

Elizabeth Warren

Our mothers always remain the strangest, craziest people we've ever met.

≯Marguerite Duras≮

Motherhood is the biggest gamble in the world. It is the glorious life force. It's huge and scary – it's an act of infinite optimism.

≫Gilda Radner≪

It's the job that I
take most seriously
in my life and
I think **it's the**
hardest job.

DEBRA MESSING

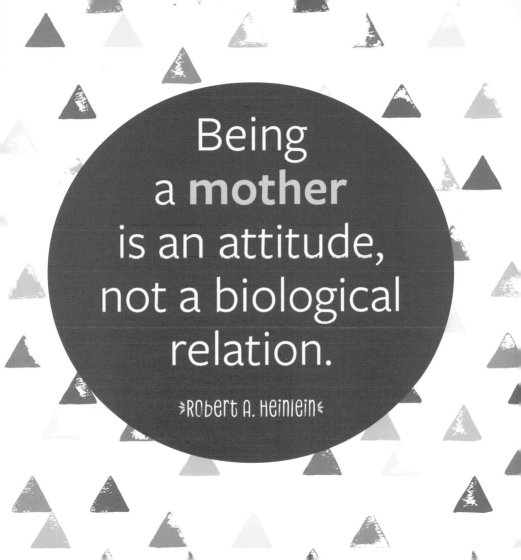

Being
a **mother**
is an attitude,
not a biological
relation.

≫Robert A. Heinlein≪

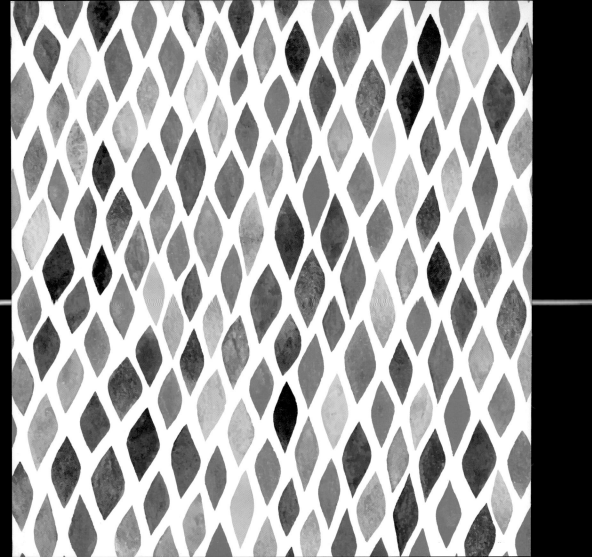

Over the years, I learned so much from **mom**. She taught me about the importance of **home** and **history** and **family** and **tradition**.

>Martha Stewart≤

If evolution really works, how come **mothers** only have two hands?

➤Milton Berle➤

A good mother
is **irreplaceable.**

≽Adriana Trigiani≼

She raised us with
humor, and she raised us
to understand that not
everything was going to
be great — but how to
laugh through it.

⊱Liza Minnelli⊰

Love
as powerful as your
mother's for you leaves
its own mark. To have
been loved so deeply …
will give us some
protection forever.

≽J.K. ROWLING≼

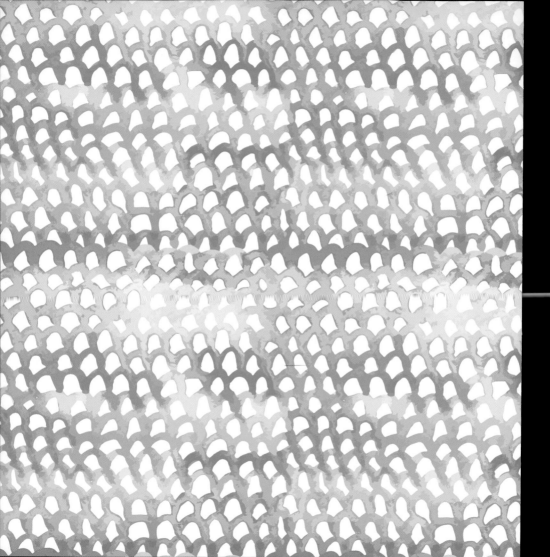

Birth is the epicenter of women's power.

⟩ANI DiFRANCO⟨

**My mother is my root,
my foundation.**
She planted the seed that
I base my life on, and that is
the belief that the ability
to achieve starts in
your mind.

>Michael Jordan<

As my mom always said, 'You'd rather have smile lines than frown lines.'

≽cindy crawford≼

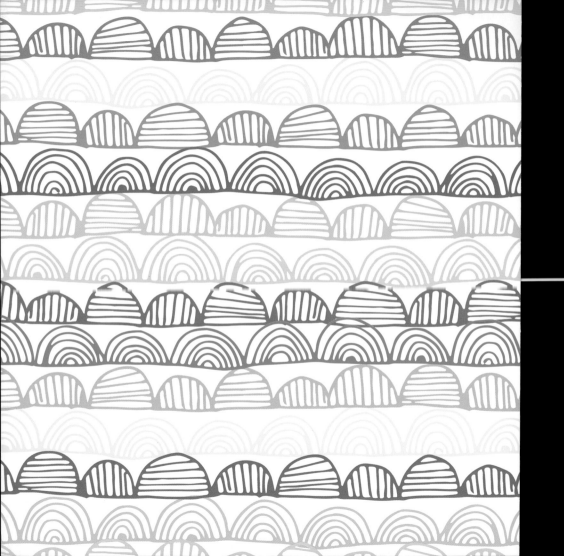

Motherhood has a very humanizing effect. Everything gets reduced to essentials.

>Meryl Streep<

Because even if the whole world was throwing rocks at you, if you still had your mother at your back, you'd be okay.

>JOJO MOYES<

A **mother** is not a person to lean on, but a person to make leaning unnecessary.

⸙DOROTHY CANFIELD FISHER⸙

Kids don't stay with you
if **you do it right**. It's the
one job where, the better
you are, the more surely
you won't be needed
in the long run.

⇒Barbara Kingsolver⇐

There's no such thing as a supermom. **We just do the best we can.**

>Sarah Michelle Gellar<

A mother's arms are more comforting than anyone else's.

⊱Princess Diana⊰

A **mother** is always the beginning. She is how things begin.

›AMY TAN‹

Having children just puts the whole world into perspective. Everything else just disappears.

⟩Kate Winslet⟨

My mom is a hard worker. She puts her head down and she gets it done. And she finds a way to have fun. She always says, 'Happiness is your own responsibility.'

⇾JENNIFER GARNER⇽

She made broken look
beautiful and strong look
invincible. She walked
with the Universe on her
shoulders and made it
look like a pair of wings.

>ARIANA DANCU<

You are amazing.

You are brave.

You are inspiring.

You are Strong as a Mother!